ELLIOT WARREN

Elliot Warren is a writer and actor from Essex. His work has been performed at Soho Theatre, National Theatre Studio, The Pleasance Theatre and Holden Street Theatre in Australia.

Flesh and Bone is his debut play. It received a Scotsman Fringe First for outstanding writing and an Overall Best Theatre Award at the Adelaide Fringe.

Elliot has also written and directed and starred in the miniseries *Stick Up*, that has gained over twelve million views online, and is being developed into a feature film.

Elliot is the co-founder of Unpolished Theatre.

Other Titles in this Series

Mike Bartlett
ALBION
BULL
GAME
AN INTERVENTION
KING CHARLES III
WILD

Tom Basden
THE CROCODILE
HOLES
JOSEPH K
THERE IS A WAR

Jez Butterworth
THE FERRYMAN
JERUSALEM
JEZ BUTTERWORTH PLAYS: ONE
MOJO
THE NIGHT HERON
PARLOUR SONG
THE RIVER
THE WINTERLING

Elinor Cook
THE GIRL'S GUIDE TO SAVING
    THE WORLD
IMAGE OF AN UNKNOWN
    YOUNG WOMAN
THE LADY FROM THE SEA *after* Ibsen
PILGRIMS

Fiona Doyle
ABIGAIL
COOLATULLY
DELUGE
THE STRANGE DEATH OF JOHN DOE

Samantha Ellis
CLING TO ME LIKE IVY
HOW TO DATE A FEMINIST

Vivienne Franzmann
BODIES
MOGADISHU
PESTS
THE WITNESS

Stacey Gregg
LAGAN
OVERRIDE
PERVE
SCORCH
SHIBBOLETH
WHEN COWS GO BOOM

Ella Hickson
THE AUTHORISED KATE BANE
BOYS
EIGHT
ELLA HICKSON PLAYS: ONE
OIL
PRECIOUS LITTLE TALENT
    & HOT MESS
WENDY & PETER PAN
    after Barrie
THE WRITER

Sam Holcroft
COCKROACH
DANCING BEARS
EDGAR & ANNABEL
PINK
RULES FOR LIVING
THE WARDROBE
WHILE YOU LIE

Vicky Jones
THE ONE
TOUCH

Anna Jordan
CHICKEN SHOP
FREAK
YEN

Lucy Kirkwood
BEAUTY AND THE BEAST
    with Katie Mitchell
BLOODY WIMMIN
CHIMERICA
HEDDA *after* Ibsen
IT FELT EMPTY WHEN THE
    HEART WENT AT FIRST BUT
    IT IS ALRIGHT NOW
LUCY KIRKWOOD PLAYS: ONE
MOSQUITOES
NSFW
TINDERBOX

Evan Placey
CONSENSUAL
GIRLS LIKE THAT
GIRLS LIKE THAT & OTHER PLAYS
    FOR TEENAGERS
JEKYLL & HYDE *after* R.L. Stevenson
PRONOUN

Sam Potter
HANNA

Stef Smith
GIRL IN THE MACHINE
HUMAN ANIMALS
REMOTE
SWALLOW

Jack Thorne
2ND MAY 1997
BUNNY
BURYING YOUR BROTHER IN
    THE PAVEMENT
A CHRISTMAS CAROL *after* Dickens
HOPE
JACK THORNE PLAYS: ONE
JUNKYARD
LET THE RIGHT ONE IN
    after John Ajvide Lindqvist
MYDIDAE
THE SOLID LIFE OF SUGAR WATER
STACY & FANNY AND FAGGOT
WHEN YOU CURE ME
WOYZECK *after* Büchner

Phoebe Waller-Bridge
FLEABAG

Elliot Warren

FLESH
AND BONE

A story created by
Elliot Warren & Olivia Brady

NICK HERN BOOKS

London

www.nickhernbooks.co.uk

A Nick Hern Book

Flesh and Bone first published in Great Britain as a paperback original in 2018 by Nick Hern Books Limited, The Glasshouse, 49a Goldhawk Road, London W12 8QP, in association with Unpolished Theatre

Flesh and Bone copyright © 2018 Elliot Warren

Elliot Warren has asserted his right to be identified as the author of this work

Cover image: © Elliot Warren

Designed and typeset by Nick Hern Books, London
Printed and bound in Great Britain by Mimeo Ltd, Huntingdon, Cambridgeshire PE29 6XX

A CIP catalogue record for this book is available from the British Library

ISBN   978 1 84842 750 1

Flesh and Bone was first performed by Unpolished Theatre at The Etcetera Theatre, London, in December 2016. In early 2017 Unpolished received the Charlie Hartill Special Reserve Fund from the Pleasance Theatre and went on to have a sell-out run at the Edinburgh Festival Fringe in 2017 at the Pleasance Theatre, where it won three awards including a *Scotsman* Fringe First for outstanding new writing. It was then developed at the National Theatre Studio before travelling to the Adelaide Fringe Festival in Australia and winning the Overall Best Theatre Award and a Critics' Circle Award. It then transferred to Soho Theatre, London, in July 2018. The cast was as follows:

TERRENCE	Elliot Warren
KELLY	Olivia Brady
REISS	Michael Jinks
GRANDAD	Nick T Frost
JAMAL	Alessandro Babalola
Directors	Elliot Warren & Olivia Brady

Introduction
Elliot Warren

Every Christmas my grandad's sister, Joanie, would throw a big old 'do' at her house in Stepney. It was one of those befitting, white townhouses around a green. It would be dark early and cars would pull up and members of the family would usher one another to the door, dressed to the nines in suits and evening dresses, greeted by an onslaught of kisses and hugs and little cheek-slaps. Think Robert De Niro in *Goodfellas*, only nobody is slipping tenners into anyone's jacket pockets.

Our family is big and no one could ever move once you were inside, we were packed tightly into the corridors, the kitchen, the living room. A riot of mini-conversations rolling into one big burble of noise, a charming cacophony of familiar voices talking and laughing over one another, all with that East London weight on the words. Slade or The Pogues are singing out over the stereo and Joanie's dishing out the most beautiful food, her famous sausages and potatoes. The lighting is warm and rich and people's faces are rosy from all the booze. Marga with her lovely big ginger hair, Steven, Tracey, Uncle Keiron and Auntie Julie and my incredible mum laughing their heads off. Lorraine, Pat and Daisy-May, Peter in his tidy get-up and Terry and Alan with his divine kindness and sensational hugs and Martin and Vicky and Sara and Jack. All these brilliant and beautiful faces, convivial and happy, that I loved to see at Christmas.

Then my grandad, Farvey Bob, would walk in, a man that can wear a dressing gown and still uphold the look of some great and suave East-End King, and I'd think, 'There's the head of the family.' In a suit with his gold jewellery, I'd feel so honoured to be that man's grandson. With Farvey came my wonderful nan and my uncles (both my age, something I shan't bother to explain), Robert and Jake, brothers to me, whom I love dearly, may Jake rest in peace. Once that lot were packed into the gaff the night was complete in my eyes.

There would be this great big present-giving ceremony where about fifty people would clamber into the living room and give out gifts, there was a richness to it all, so much character in one bustling environment. I don't think there was ever a moment of silence.

We would leave, late, I'd be in the car next to my mum or whoever was the designated driver, asleep, rolling through London at night in December, with Tony Bennett playing quietly on the radio.

The spectacular energy those parties accomplished keeps those memories so vivid for me. They had such a profound and touching effect.

Thanks to my family I've always wanted to write about the array of characters the East End spawns.

The first draft of *Flesh and Bone* was written in a month inside mine and Olivia's bedroom in Dalston. With it came our theatre company too, Unpolished Theatre. We had booked The Etcetera, Camden, before pen was put to paper so we needed to get cracking as we gave ourselves two months to get the whole thing done, dusted and on stage.

We were auditioning actors in our 'lovely' kitchen before the script was anywhere near finished, with one elderly chap telling me my writing made no sense which was terrifying at the time as nobody else had seen the bloody thing! We made almost every actor a cuppa when they entered, and Olivia and I upheld the pretence that we knew precisely what we were doing at all times.

The second month was for rehearsals. I pulled in favours left, right and centre to get rehearsal spaces, cracking PR shots, a trailer, a top-notch illustrator and I did all of the marketing myself. I became Unpolished Theatre's self-professed hype-man, plastering social media with our black, white and orange pictures I'd knocked up. The whole thing went quickly and our two-week run at The Etcetera felt like standing atop a mountain, even if there was the odd night with only two or three audience members...

The following year, 2017, a deluge of opportunities were there to be seized. We fought hard and received the Pleasance Theatre's Charlie Hartill Fund which took us to the Edinburgh Fringe. It was there where we performed with so much gusto, passion and energy that we won a Scotsman Fringe First for outstanding new writing, a sell-out show award and an award to perform at the Adelaide Fringe Festival, which meant we got to jet off to Australia in 2018. Returning to London, we got to develop the show at the National Theatre Studios and secured a transfer to Soho Theatre. It all felt a long way away from the intimate confides of The Etcetera with our modest audiences.

It's been a ride, a white-knuckle one, corkscrewing at full-throttle through the outskirts and into the hustle and bustle of an industry I want to keep climbing. I have never been more proud of a piece of work than this one yet. Just like my family of East-Enders, the characters in this play come alive with rollicking beauty and we fought hard to be seen and heard every time we fired out onto the stage, something that lends itself to the attitude of this play.

My grandad saw the show, sat right at the bloody front with his walking stick, in his suit, with all his gold on. Afterwards, he came out and he said: 'How the bleedin' hell did you write all that, boy?'

Thanks

To my mum, Anne Murtaugh, for your unlimited love and for bigging up the play to anyone with a pair of ears, even when there was only a couple of sentences.

To my dad, Warren Murtaugh, for the phone calls packed with advice, ideas and inspiration.

To Clodagh Wallace and Judith Tunstall for the love, support and for that fateful evening that made all of this possible.

To Sue Odell for your persistent belief, your unwaivering optimism and your support.

To Alessandro Babalola, Nick T Frost and Michael Jinks for your exceptional work and infinite confidence in this show.

To the Pleasance Theatre and their Charlie Hartill Fund for believing in the show and taking us to the Edinburgh Festival Fringe. Especially Anthony Alderson and the fantastic Heather Rose, you are the business.

To the Acting Tutors of the Arts University Bournemouth who taught us to stand up and be counted for within this gigantic industry.

And to the incredibly multitalented Olivia Brady for creating this world and this story with me.

E.W.

For my grandad, Farvey Bob,
and the rest of my beautiful family

Characters

TERRENCE
KELLY
REISS
GRANDAD
JAMAL

Notes on Text

This text is an extended version of the original play.

The following is performed with bestial fire. You will take on
these souls with spirit. Taste every word, wear their despairs,
revel in their delights, these vigorous vibes must be pronounced
with a sharp tongue and an even flow. Embody them with salient
showmanship for now be the time these dregs will articulate their
calamities. A breed seen as unfit for vocation will deliver with
gusto, you will rattle the house in which you play.

*This text went to press before the end of rehearsals and so may
differ slightly from the play as performed.*

Prologue

What a Piece of Work is a Man

A central spotlight. Smoke hangs in the air. A low rumble of guttural noise.

The stage is empty.

TERRENCE, *wild-eyed yet ostensibly poised, takes centre stage.*

The nerves around his eye twitch as he observes the audience with dangerous intent.

Our characters speak with virile eloquence.

TERRENCE. What a piece of work is a man. A beast of many forms, traits, ideas. Power maketh man, Greed maketh man. Man maketh love, desire, hate, fear and lust. Money maketh man, today. Without coinage how does one expect to survive? Down in the gutter, deep down what where people don't like to talk about that's where I reside, my life is led boldly where no nancy wants to stroll. Step lightly around these ends my friends, for this is East London where the villains do rock and roll...

REISS. Behold! A band of creatures with wicked woes whose problems you probably care none too about.

KELLY. But prickling problems none the less for the less fortunate in our land, whose lives are obscure to the hordes of the norm.

JAMAL. A rotten shitstorm of concrete housing, no signs of architectural design, just bricks and mortar that rise high.

GRANDAD. This fabulous delight which offends the eye is quite the sight, and the setting for our play, where this assembly of souls do reside.

TERRENCE. So, prick up thine ears and gird firmly into your stalls, great house of hearers! Gawk our gritty assemblage of geezers and birds for now be the time to give attention to these folk, to turn a blind one to the blatant and realise that we are all just flesh and that we are all just bone!

The recalcitrant gang now presented before us look upon their audience with menace. They roar and charge forward but immediately break into chaotic dance, all wild grins and flailing limbs, as big-band, swinging music erupts and gushes into the next scene.

Scene One

The Boozer

REISS. Now here be a monster! A savage, a fork-tongued devil of barbaric proportions. A villainous character who goes by the name of Terrence, Terry or Tel, whichever you prefer coz he ain't that fussed.

TERRENCE. I ain't that fussed.

REISS. Tel's lady friend is Kel, Kelly to some but to me usually Kel, for one syllable is easier to yell when one has run out of paper on the shitter. Kel is a corker. I'm that dastardly crooked fellow's brother, and my name is Reiss, you cannot really shorten Reiss like Terry so that is that. My brother and I live alongside his soon-to-be wife and her grandad. This foursome did not choose this life, for we be poor and must squash together under one roof so that our bills do get paid on time. Now, below our sorry little box within which we reside is –

TERRENCE. The Lion!

EVERYONE. The Boozer!

TERRENCE. Our Church for better a word!

REISS. A red-bricked Mecca, where there was never a queue.

TERRENCE. Gold did flow, darts were thrown and dogs were allowed in too.

REISS. Because John behind the bar was a fucking legend, he understood that animals had feelings just like me and you.

TERRENCE. We were sat in the corner it was a dreary noon some Tuesday a while back.

The music abruptly halts and switches to some muted sports commentary playing in the foreground. GRANDAD *takes on the role of 'John the Barman'.*

REISS. The Hammers were spanking Millwall three–nil, Tel was ordering a pint of something German, a pale ale for his missus and a packet of dry-roasted nuts, lovely!

TERRENCE. Fucked – I was, as John had poured the bastards and I was two nick short.

REISS. My pockets were dry from the other night, a round of chicken and chips for silly bollocks and his soon-to-be wife –

TERRENCE. I gave Reiss a dejected look.

REISS. He looked out of sorts, but what the fuck could I do?

TERRENCE. Sorry John pal I'm two nick short, how aboutcha turn a blind one and I give it to yah tomorrow day?

GRANDAD. Ney!

REISS. He spat.

TERRENCE. I winced, I licked my teeth, did this cunt want beef? Just keep the poxy peace and let me leave with my pint, my ale and my fucking nuts. Fore I ram my fist into that rotund belly of yours and pull out your rotten fucking guts!

REISS. John looked at Tel through glazed over eyes. He's heard it all before…

GRANDAD. Liberty-taking bastards we should charge at the door.

TERRENCE. Half past bloody four, ain't even had me scampi and chips and my pockets are penniless. I'm fuming, I'm marching about like a minotaur trapped in its murky labyrinth, when Kel, my lovely sweet Kelly Baby gel with her lovely arse jumps up and hollers:

KELLY. Fuck me a score! Look babe a fucking twenty in me bag!

TERRENCE. That fucking slag!

KELLY. Drinks are on me, get me some scampi! You can have the chips I'm on a diet.

TERRENCE. There you are John you massive bell-end, I want my change and I'll have three plates of scampi and a mountain of thinly cut, deep-fried potatoes thank you good sir. I wrapped my fingers rand my icey chalice and neck a good chunk of golden fluid.

GRANDAD. You're still two pound shy.

TERRENCE. What! Why? I spat, glass in hand like a caveman's tool.

GRANDAD. Scampi's a fiver, with chips that's six, your pint is four, your ale is four and fifty pence and those nuts set you back another two. YOU – who gave me six and a fifty pence and your missus that score, I need two pound more or OP IT.

REISS. Shit a fucking pig John, Tel don't take kindly to torment.

KELLY. His face curled gargoyle-like. An almighty strain did invade his nut, flush with fury I did spot a vein, with girth like a whale, begin to pulsate.

TERRENCE. I raised my chalice in the air and threw it, hard, across the bar... Where it met with an unfortunate soul named Jamal. Hard as nails, with a screw loose like myself.

REISS. Now, Jamal and our lot went back a fair way, played in the car park with shit on sticks on hot summer days, not no more though, we grew out of that, now Terrence and Jamal like to scrap, almost lovingly like, but probably not.

JAMAL. AH! Who dare disturb my quiet pint before work? Tel you shit, I'll stab you in your eye and have my way with your bitch!

TERRENCE. Shit.

REISS. Do I defend my brother and fight to the death or do I take Kel back to Grandad at the flat, smoke a joint and fall into bed?

TERRENCE. Reiss, take my hand let's fend off this fork-tongued cunt together, stand proud on our sacred land.

REISS. So I did band, brothers united, side by side to fend off this beast, this snarling monster, Jamal the Cyclops.

The brothers rib and taunt JAMAL, *who bites back. Heaps of testosterone is batted back and forth.*

KELLY. John was slapping the bar, tantrum-like, something spewed from his ugly chops about –

GRANDAD. Not in this bar you won't!

JAMAL hurls a beer bottle at TERRENCE *and* REISS *and it smashes behind them on the wall. Everyone suspends the chaos for a brief moment of disbelief and then* TERRENCE *reaches for a chair and heaves it in* JAMAL's *direction. The fight is instantly slowed down, everything played out in half speed.*

Mozart begins, 'Piano Concerto No. 21'.

KELLY. Tables turnt, bar stools swam the flood of stale air like giant insects, Jamal rose and swung his bear paw across the bar top and it crashed into several wines and pints.

Glass flies, cracks and splinters, causing tiny explosions of razor-sharp shards.

A large triangular piece meets with John's cheek, rouge rushes, claret all over the deck, slice, a bloody mess.

REISS. Tel and I are blind to the crime, side by side, as we proceed towards the giant Jamal.

TERRENCE. I wrap my fingers round to create a smashing device and lift it high above me head.

REISS. Tel looked wild, like a barbarian at war, I watched as his fist hit down on to Jamal's head.

KELLY. Cracked it did like an egg.

JAMAL crashes to the deck. The music stops and everything catches up with itself, we are in real time again.

REISS. His eyes rolled about, and we thought that David had triumphed over the great Goliath… But nay, it angered the beast some more.

The family huddle together whilst JAMAL *gets to his feet, in a moment of panic, disorder and chaos,* TERRENCE *runs towards the gigantic* JAMAL *who holds out his hands and wraps them around* TERRENCE*'s neck, who is then lifted off of his feet.*

JAMAL. I grabbed at this little prick's throat and dug my fingers deep, You peasant, you BUMBACLAT, you fool!

KELLY. In all his valour, with his most mightily efforts, Tel did roar…

TERRENCE manages a pathetic nothing of a noise. He is thrown to the ground and instantly goes for JAMAL*, the scene slows again, apart from each narrator.*

REISS. I reckon he would have tried to slew this bastard back, whereby Jamal would have broken Tel's sorry little back, so the fact he was choking was helping the twat – a Catch-22 I'd say?

KELLY. For christ's sake do summin Reiss, please!

REISS. Fuck me… A shiny pint by my side I reached for this killing device.

KELLY. SMACK.

The scene thumps into real time again.

He thumped it across Jamal's head – right round the back, the big twat flopped ard and released Tel, the little fucktard.

TERRENCE. The place was a war zone of wicked proportion. Kel was on her feet, scampi tucked in a cloth, I grab my nuts and wink at my brother, what a legend, what a boss.

REISS. I cock my head towards the door, Kel whips round the table and we leave this sorry sight.

TERRENCE. This ruckus, this rowdy royal rumble of primitive delights, all on a Tuesday, in the broad daylight…

GRANDAD. And don't forget karaoke on Saturday night!

Blackout.

TERRENCE *rushes offstage,* JAMAL *jumps to his feet and exits. The big-band music closes the scene in one final moment of swinging revelry.*

Scene Two

Brigitte Bardot

KELLY *appears in a spotlight.*

KELLY. Like a deep and darkly hole with which there is no foreseeable bottom, my woes see no end. This part I play, this face I pretend, puts pallisades between reality and what emits from my not-so-decorous defence. But I ain't no damsel in distress, be sure about that, fuckers. I swim with the sharks, play ball in the lion's den. You see, round these trenches I am a foot soldier in a ceaseless war we will both win and lose in the end.

What say you then? Smirk go on, call me: Silly, naive, weak. I'm a survivor on a busy island, where there ain't much left to eat.

You see, there ain't no time to close my eyes and picture a brighter horizon. I love to belt out musical sounds from my mouth, and I ain't too bad at it neither. Alas, it is a damming shame that this passion lay to waste, that the air I blow to and fro my vocal chords must remain but a hidden talent… For this wasteland I do strut upon costs an almighty sum to keep. Knee-deep in shit, I wade through the grime and the grit.

And so you ponder, how does this barbarian find a pretty penny, with no GCSEs or any sign of an educated mind? What actions can acquire mintage for a girl stuck in a debauched sewer which be so utterly fixated on ladily assets? Well it was obvious to me, after one or two cups of tea, sat on Stacey's settee, when she spat: 'Kelly! Baby! You can earn a fat little wedge! Do you know how many men would part ways with their coins to hear your little voice.' And she did show me the pot at the end of the rainbow friends. And I will let you in on this lucrative secret, for I have cracked the nut! Ladies, open those ears and come in close, for we be sipping now on the most costly of rosé wines: 'Sex Chatlines.' A world in which blokes be led by their members, where those morons go to explode in archaic ecstasy, exploitation be the name of the game girls and those unshapely sacks of skin dun arf spend a fortune...

GRANDAD *appears in an opposing spotlight.*

GRANDAD. Insatiable, voracious, wolfish and ravenous delight for the ladies I possess, but I do stress I ain't no pervert thinking about these little birds getting undressed no, no, I am a gentleman – yes I ponder upon the odd tit now and then – but I feed from the need to charm and excite. See I reside from a time, many decades ago, where a geezer would dress nice, in a whistle and flute, his hair would be combed and there'd be some tasty shoes fixing him to the ground on which he would strut. Class it was. These days, my unwiped ass has more sodding class than these dirty, rotten scrubs waving their dicks about the pubs and clubs. It's a forgotten art, is class.

I could sit and spill some amorous tales from where and when I met my darling wife, but, ho, I won't for I worry that I would get teary-eyed, as that lovely fair-haired bird, love of my life, she went and died.

I tell you this, that is when life, it went and dived, plummeted fast and hard into shallow water, but remained did I and so I picked up the mangled pieces and put them together again, Frankenstein-like, and what remained there after was a very lonely geezer.

An old oak in a deadened field. From that day on something changed, golem-like my skin became, tough, I was rigid, stiff with unjustly hate for this rock on which I still sat. Bitten by some foul and ugly emotion... It stung; it left a lump and would not wilt so easily. And in my tortured and pitiful state, dragging my darkly cloud around I fell into a hole, with no hand to help me out. A right pickle I had gotten my little self into my friends. I could see no end. Until, down in The Lion I met with Paddy, a friend from days ago, who told me all about the girls he found in the back of the *Hackney Gazette*. At first I spat out my mouthful of pint and said 'You're having a fucking giraffe!' But look I did do and, fuck me, found did I.

KELLY. From my boudoir, I lay atop my sheets, like a Frenchy getting painted I run a finger cross my cheek, pushing myself up and down, escaping sounds, you could drown, I writhe and sway, my body aches. I can ease your search through the darkness as you sit, gripped to your manhood, swelling with frustration. Dial my digits and let me climb aboard, for I am an articulate Aphrodite sent through the wires to melt your sword.

All lies! I sit on the sofa fucking bored, watching reruns of *The Bill*, eating packets of Haribo, scratching my arse, waiting to be called – by one of these dirty little pervs so I can make a few quid.

Here's one now, making funny sounds, got this little accent of the box, posh-like, snotty type. It was that lovely Joanna Lumley spouting some nonsense one Sunday morn when I was eating some 'cheese on', was ogling her mouth and the way it wrapped its tongue round those syllables. 'Hi darling.' Weren't arf bad at it by the time Tel came home with a carrier of Morley's golden bird and chips, 'Are you there big boy?' sends these sorry sods sailing it does. Blokes, fucking oafs mostly ain't they.

GRANDAD. I scoured the papers to find what fitted me; it didn't take long to come across the perfect one. Posh little bird said she resided west, and oh did we connect. The soft modes of expression in her airy tone sent shrills of joy through the phone and into my blood. Causing me to instantly stand to attention, a rarity at my ripe old age. It was love again, my friends! Hallelujah! I wore my old and rumpled skin only as a cloak, for what I spoke, what I gave to her verbally, was class, charisma, heart. I felt young once more! Eternal youth! 'Ermmm, uhm-uhm, ello darlin how've you been?' Gotta keep it smooth.

KELLY. 'Stiffen up, I'm climbing aboard.' I get straight to the point with this fella, he's a dirty little regular, get him shooting quick so I've got time before *Corrie* to have a shit.

GRANDAD. 'Oh yep, okay, yes sweetie, I'm all yours.' This little darlin' transports me she does, I see her as Brigitte Bardot, arching her back, legs akimbo.

KELLY. I'm prancing about the kitchen, wondering what to unfreeze for our banquet that eve, whilst singing 'Fuck yes, big boy, fuck, fuck, fucking yes please!'

GRANDAD. Oh you goddess, you angel, you epitome of beauty, don't stop, fill this void, I want you truly!

KELLY. 'Oh god yes. You make me so wet.' I lie to this sack as he comes to a glorious end.

GRANDAD *is in ecstasy,* KELLY*, meanwhile, is filing down her nails.*

GRANDAD. Oh jesus christ you in arf special!

KELLY. Oh yes baby, am I?

GRANDAD. Oh God, say summink French!

KELLY. French?

GRANDAD. French!

KELLY. Ermm… croissant?

GRANDAD. Ohhhh, pot pourri!

KELLY. Oh you naughty man!

GRANDAD. Yes I am!

KELLY. Oh yeh!

GRANDAD. FUCK!

KELLY. YES –

GRANDAD. SHIT!

KELLY. YES –

GRANDAD. TITS!

KELLY. YES –

GRANDAD. FUCK!

KELLY. YES –

GRANDAD. FUUUUUUUUCCCKKKK…

He climaxes, he doubles over and his eyes roll about his head until he lets out a grotesque and awkward moan, we ride this cringe-worthy wave as his voice breaks and his body convulses five or six times.

You know what… I love you –

KELLY. WOAH. I cut off before I hear that shit. Sometimes I catch it and I gag a little bit. Alas, that was a worthy six-minute conversation, easiest score I'll ever make, ey. Grandad?

A long pause, whereby both characters are sorting themselves out.

GRANDAD!

GRANDAD. What?

KELLY. Your dinner's on your plate!

GRANDAD. Ang on a bleedin minute!

KELLY. What you doin in there?

GRANDAD. What d'you care! Mind your own soddin business!

Goodbye my secret lover… Until next time!

GRANDAD *and* KELLY *exit.*

Scene Three

The Sticky Black Treacle

REISS *takes centre stage.*

REISS. Be I a canvas for some dilettante? An experiment
whereby nobody knows the aims or outcomes? I am but a
singularity round my ends, friends. An anomaly round here.
You see, I am young and in my prime, a brand-new twenty-
five ladies and gents, a contented and joyful life I lead, but
lead it I cannot all of the time.

For, since I was a youngen, I have been a product of a merrily
miserable life, a nasty, evil, villainous path I have always
walked upon, alongside my brother Terrence we sweep the
night frolicking kicking people's heads in, drinking in the
boozer and scraping our cash together by delving into shady
deals, those are the cards I was dealt people. Like a sticky
black treacle I cannot – no must not – pull myself out of this
murk. For I be Billy the little Goats Gruff and I must not cross
that bridge to the green, green grass for my big brother, the
cockney troll, will spank my ass.

And yet, I do cross that bridge now and then for Terrence
and me are not joined at the hip, or if you think we are, it be
glue not skin, so I do rip apart every so often. What awaits
me, wait – awakens me – whence I'm over there, could
never be spoken about here in the treacle that is my estate.
For over there are lights and dancing, colourful pills that spin
you about, music so loud your ears ring forever, and boys, so
many boys...

What? What is it? You believe that my character be only
keen to court the opposing sex?

It be like this...

A club song begins and REISS *speaks with new-found libido
and passion, his voice holding on to every word as he
recounts his workplace.*

I am employed to pour poisons into fancy-shaped glasses, in
good old Soho I spend my time behind a neon bar, I am stuff

of legend round those parts. I've had every Brando in that
sector and I am ogled upon like a god. Honestly, a fucking
Zeus before their hungry eyeballs. It be a few moons past
since I did acquire this position, would collect jars from the
noisy floor where chaps would dance. Grasped on the ass
I would be all the poxy time, daggers I'd throw them and
wrestle my way through the colourful horde. You see I was
con-fuddled, I had never had a bloke, never realised this
certitude about me, until a Fridee, bout half past three there
was this lad, standing before me, gallantly, like fucking Jimmy
Dean in his rosy red bomber. Cool he was, didn't give one
fucketh, you know? I worshiped this arctic monkey. Twas
minutes after I made myself apparent that we did punch lips.

REISS *lunges forward and kisses him.*

I wrestled this demigod off and struck his pretty boat! 'Go
prick thy face and over-red thy fear thou lily-livered boy!'

But, oh folly was that strike, you see, retrospectively, with
the brain that swims the juices in my head today; I should
have stayed, made something with that boy...

If you haven't cottoned on yet, I'll spell it out for you, over the
bridge be Soho town and I turn into a massive homosexual.
Like a man of Sparta, I have unconditional love for my
endowed brothers, a reflection on my behaviour thine virile
sibling would oppose, most certainly. Not sure why? I mean
can a fella not be a geezer and be fabulous at the same time?

Work unlocks this truity about me. But I diminish on my bus
ride back to my abode; for I cannot speak of my true self back
at home. See the life I lead is merrily miserable indeed, that's
me; I was born and raised in that block and fight for my
existence I must. I do not have time, should not be devoting
energy to forming my own personality it will only get me
stuffed in the end... And the end is always nigh round here.

I fear one day, intoxicated, I will spill. Tell Terrence and Kel,
Grandad too, the frightful truth about me, I do worry so, that
they would abandon me...

You know, in order to keep that fear at bay I drown in fumes,
I smoke a fat one most nights so I do sleep soundly. I pick up
from Jamal, once a week usually, now that's a chap I'd
delightfully fuck. What a treat to the eyeballs that almighty
figure be. Can you imagine the size of it? (*Whistles*.) No, nor
can I, our tiny minds cannot comprehend something of that
size. I turn up awkward-like. Fidgeting, restless… high.
Alright?

We are slung into JAMAL'*s world now, a hip-hop or grime
beat plays out from* JAMAL'*s flat.*

JAMAL. Reiss my lickle badman, what say you fam?

REISS. Oh not much just been (Having a wank over you my
friend) watching telly.

JAMAL. What be the weight of our exchange this week?

REISS. An ounce please.

JAMAL. Sweet.

REISS. I grit my teeth, I can't be seen being a queen round here.
Although every inch of my existence would burst if Jamal
were to invite me inside for a smoke on his pipe. If you know
what I mean… Listen, Jamal my old friend, it's a bit short my
end, only got a bull's-eye, can I pay you next week?

JAMAL. Your word is good Reiss so away with you, but be
there no money in my hand by next week, I will grab you by
the balls and squeeze, part them from your groin and watch
you bleed.

REISS. Yes please.

JAMAL *grabs* REISS *by the scruff of the neck and for
a second to long they are very close together, almost
touching noses,* REISS *gets off on this.* JAMAL *lets him go
with confusion.*

Scene Four

I Be Dante

JAMAL *is left centre stage alone, he looks upon the audience, out at all the faces staring back at him. He stands very still and straight.*

Chopin's 'Nocturne No. 20 in C-sharp minor' plays delicately as our villain begins his soliloquy.

JAMAL. This stench upon my house, this wicked life I must lead, from things I've been witness too, to the things I've seen upon my TV. I sell to the demons that walk these streets and my heart bleeds for the weak, but manz gotta eat.

I just play the part that was given to me in this fierce and odious game. I wear my chainmail boldly, and haunt the darkest parts of this estate, for I have a lot of shit on my plate and ain't not one soul trying to be my mate, ain't not one creature eager to see me for more than just a dealer. Ain't not one of you know my pain.

The piece of music cuts.

Yo, where you from? Where do your colours run?

I be Dante, this land on which I stand be my inferno, my netherworld whereby I reside. This abyss, this concrete nothingness, I have made my home, grown to hold dear that which others may fear. I live here, these blocks of stone be my unholy ends, and so? What shall come from a place so foul? Monsters I hear you howl. Devils you shout. The dregs that will stay snared and never get out.

If I rolled up on an establishment in town, looking somehow to make some coinage to feed my mother, I would set my credentials down before the big man, in his starched white shirt and name tag stamped 'Kevin' he will roll his eyeballs up and down until my estate's proverbial name is found. Then a gulping sound will fill out the silence, Kevin will carefully look upon my furrowed brow and in his most pleasant tone of voice, stutter out:

'Sorry sir, we aren't taking any vacancies at the minute.'

I snatch back my ball and chain, my heavy weight that I carry around beside my name. This is the way I live. So what now? I stay in the pits and drown because of it.

See, tis unlikely for me to set my feet anywhere but this hellhole, so to make ends meet I must sell narcotics to the zombies that fall behind me on these streets, don't blame me, blame yourselves, you created this place, you gave it its unholy name by treating us like dogs.

So come see me if you seek a herbal remedy, help me treat my sick mother, grab a twenty bag from a brother.

JAMAL *leaves and the next scene spills into his exit.*

Scene Five

The Rat Ballet

GRANDAD *takes a seat and turns on the football.* REISS *enters and after watching for a second heads to his room, which is on* GRANDAD's *shoulder.* KELLY *enters and leans over* GRANDAD's *head, where the kitchen is set.* TERRENCE *is last to enter, who uses* GRANDAD's *other shoulder as the toilet, he picks up the newspaper and begins to read the sports section. We are shown how cramped this family really are.*

KELLY. Terrence, do you want a tea?

TERRENCE. Ey?

KELLY. Do you wanna cup of tea?

TERRENCE. I can't hear yah!

KELLY. Christ, tea! Do you want a bloody tea!

TERRENCE. Tea?

KELLY. Yes!

TERRENCE. Yeah, I'll have a tea.

KELLY. Christ almighty…

GRANDAD. I'll have a brew!

KELLY. I know you will.

> KELLY *awkwardly leans over* GRANDAD *and uses*
> TERRENCE*'s back to put down the mugs, she makes the*
> *teas with great strain, circumscribed to her cramped*
> *confines.* REISS *begins to lift weights in his room, working*
> *his biceps. The footy on the TV gains some pace and*
> GRANDAD *is watching on tenterhooks.* TERRENCE *is*
> *reading the paper and anticipating a rather sensitive bowel*
> *movement. The cacophony they all begin to create rises and*
> *bottlenecks, tightly, into a disarray of noises. Then it*
> *explodes, a goal is scored on the box,* REISS *strains to reach*
> *his final rep,* TERRENCE *doubles over in agony and*
> KELLY *screams wildly for she has just noticed a rat shuffle*
> *out from underneath the sink and shift across the kitchen.*

TERRENCE. I was having a Richard one Sunday morn when
Kel was screwing from near the kitchen.

GRANDAD. Screaming she was, my earholes could have bled,
drowning out the box with her bloody noise.

REISS. That said, she was well within her rights to be shaking
the lights with her lungs. For a fat black rat was gnawing
through the trash with its equally repulsive relative.

KELLY. Tel you bastard, that's that kebab you left unwrapped
that's done that!

TERRENCE. Ey?

KELLY. Come in ere and bring your fuckin baseball bat!

TERRENCE. I stayed sat, unsure what she was piping up for
until from under the shitter, right there on the fucking floor,
a dirty bloody rat went racing past and under the door. I shot
up, unwiped and boxers round ankles, I wobbled out the water
closet and I did see a fucking army of rats storming the flat.

GRANDAD. Jesus fucking christ what's this all about!

KELLY. Grandad spat as one of the bastard rats climbed up his back and took a chunk from his head!

GRANDAD. Shit a pig!

REISS. Methinks I know exactly what this is… Jamal!

JAMAL. What!

REISS. Anything particularly out of the ordinary going on up there?

JAMAL. Yeh!

REISS. What?

JAMAL. Fucking rodents in the fridge!

KELLY *and* TERRENCE. Kill it!

REISS. Methinks I know exactly what this is!

You see this lovely system-built social housing of the sixties is quite the eyesore, particularly foul for the middle-class dog-walkers on their dreary morning out-and-aboutings. You see, me thinks the highest council of our lovely area wants us gone, sharpish! Would be tickety-fucking-boo with blowing this bastard up and shitting on all of our shoddy little lives who are left living here. Me thinks those bastards have planted this plague! Those mercilessly callous cunts! We be the pawns in their game of chess, friends, just a piece to be destroyed to make way for the wealthy girls and boys!

'God Save the Queen' gathers behind REISS *and lifts up his impassioned rant.*

I'm sick of it! I'm not having it, we need to get fucked off, we need to be enlightened, we need passion, we need vigour, we need to be royally pissed with these halfwits, we need to stand and fight for our land, Tel get your shoes on, spray some deodorant, we're storming the gates, we're not having it no more! Let us sweep the floor with those suits, let us rip the heads from their necks and shout down into what's left, 'You will not turf us from our land!'

TERRENCE. Reiss!

Music cuts.

Will you shut up and give me a hand, Grandad's having an asthma attack!

REISS. Yeah alright, but then we'll do something yeh?

TERRENCE. What?

REISS. Nothing.

KELLY. Terrence will you discard of these, please!

TERRENCE. Jesus woman! You are doing my nut in, Right! Step aside.

Strauss's 'Radetzky March' begins. TERRENCE *rushes forward and drives his foot straight down on top of a rat. Battle ensues against the army of rodents with the grace of a dancer but the bloodlust of a barbarian.*

As the others commentate, TERRENCE's *actions become wildly stylised. With what appears to be ballet fused with anarchic energy and primitive savagery, he rips off the rodents' heads using his teeth, he throws them across the room and smashes them into one another, then he begins to shoot down the rats with an array of imaginary weaponry. The rest of the family narrate his ferocious behaviour.*

REISS. Wild-eyed once more, my brother, like Vlad the Impaler, wreaks a war on our four-legged friends.

GRANDAD. Battering the little buggers to a pulp, they fly about the living room bursting open like cannon fire.

REISS. It feels oddly fulfilling watching Tel giving out pain to these little assholes that had taken reign, retribution towards the council for mucking about with our flat.

KELLY. I was proud of my herculean chap. Like bloody John Rambo he was, from off the box, such a delight to watch, tasty fucker. And, Reiss may spill some yawnful shite sometimes, but his theory on this, light bulbs did switch in my head.

REISS. It was like Terrence was beating the utter balls out of those rats for all of us. The veins protruding atop his angry nut did beat and pulse for the entire flat.

KELLY. The unapologetic smashing machine to our hungry spirits. There's one near the telly KILL IT!

TERRENCE, *roaring at the top of his lungs, makes his way around the room smashing the rats into a bloody soup atop the carpet. They begin to advance on him. During these final lines he unhooks a shotgun that is hung above the fireplace and starts to fill it with shells. In the final moment,* TERRENCE *aims and fires. The rest of the family scarper and he is left in a chaotic and violent picture, the aftermath of a bloody war, he sits victorious, blood over his face, with a huge grin.*

Scene Six

Fighting

TERRENCE. Kill the fatted calf! Raise your goblets friends and enemies for this is a toast to bloodshed!

I like to fight. I always have and I always will. It's an incessant and primitive delight inside my bestial mind.

Methinks it started from a tender age of nine, I kicked seven shades of shit out of a little git named Gregory for he called my brother a bender, fairness to say Reiss would tuck his pecker between his legs and prance, gaily, about the football pitch like a miniature lady, however, he is my flesh and blood and Gregory the little toerag would not quit, so I did hit that git in the back of the nut with a large stick. I was expelled rather quick, tossed aside by the system like a sucked orange, and thus, right there, my fiery nature was fed. In every plight and quandary I found myself seeing fucking red.

It has dug its burly knuckles into my back my whole life, has
fighting, I admit, caused pain to people I like. Take my soon-
to-be wife, Kel, in a circular hell, rotating with myself as
I have an unfortunate nack at getting the sack. I recall, a few
years back, I worked one's fingers to the bone in a little
establishment left of the high road called Mick's, a shoddy
little garage whereby cars would roll inside to get fixed, now
Mick, the harmless little prune he be… was a right jobsworth
cunt! I was required to break my back for a pittance, to slog
away nine to five every weekday, now have you ever heard of
such utter nonsense? Every poxy minute of every poxy hour
of every poxy day that geezer wanted a fucking cup of Rosie.

Watcha Tel, make us a cuppa tea will yah boy.

I beg your pardon Mick?

Just chuck the kettle on, I'm parched.

Fuck off, you've got arms.

Cheeky bastard! Did my earholes just deceive me?

What's that you just called me?

Come on son, you've done fuck-all and it's half past three,
I'll have a touch a milk and I like it sugary.

Stick your tea up your arse! I'm busy!

Are you winding me up Terry?

Seriously, Mick…

I'm not asking for a fucking picnic!

Right that's fuckin it!

Alas, I waved goodbye to Mick's little enterprise, after
throttling the cunt for calling me a word which means me old
man and his bird were not married when they gave birth.
Now, it's true, I don't know the geezer that used his sperm to
make half of what you see here now, but that don't mean any
Tom, Dick and Harry can have a say on it! Does it!

I have wrestled many times this villainous mind of mine, to
bite one's lip before I lead with a fist. A martial art be the

way for you my son! I hear the mob yell, pitchforked and
ready to lynch, hone that fury into sportsmanship! Look, be
I a billionaire, then yeh, perhaps the obvious would glare,
alas, I do not have a sack of gold each month to spare,
otherwise, yeah, I be up there, with all the greats in
guillotines, my name in lights, millions every fight, the
octagon be my house of prayer, yeh... amongst others as
mad as march hares!

Though woe is me, for this land on which I stand is turning
to rubble, Kel longs to decamp this unfruitful ground, but
that shall cost a fair penny.

Alas, it got me to scratching my nut... Seeing as my expertise
are of the fighting kind would it not be wise to delve into an
enterprise that would support my wicked ways. So, that is why
I did get friendly with the lovely Jamal as I knew he was of
the same ilk, organised crime now that would run smooth as
silk. Lots of cash to be had with us two side by side. So
swallow pride we did do, banded together, an unlikely crew
we became, and our first escapade was to pillage... an offie!

During those final lines, TERRENCE *pulls ladies' tights
from his pocket and puts them over his face.* JAMAL *runs on
with his very own pair.*

JAMAL. 'Give us this day our daily bread!'

TERRENCE. Jamal said with an unholy spout of clout, out
came the contents of this fellow's coinbox and Jamal, the
bastard, snatched it up and was swiftly in and out within a
matter of moments! Let's just say I wasn't over the fucking
moon that my newly found partner had swooped in and
stolen the spotlight. Held the replica gun and he said all the
fucking words! Therefore in a sudden urge to do something
more I clenched my fist and I did hit the merchant before me
on his great-big-fat-fucking-nose!

TERRENCE *winds up a punch and holds it in midair, ready
to drive it into the imaginary merchants face. Chopin's
'Nocturne No. 20 in C-sharp minor, Op. 9' begins and the
gang run onto the stage like sugar plum fairies at the ballet.*

They all form a crest around TERRENCE *and mimic the punch. Then, the entire gang descend onto the merchant in slow motion.*

The punch connects and the chorus break off from TERRENCE *with a racket that apes the dastardly deed, taking the form of a moving, macabre Michelangelo painting.* TERRENCE *watches the merchant fly backwards in agony and an overwhelming sense of accomplishment floods him.*

And as bone did split and blood did spit I thought for a bit that I had seen the most beautiful scene on this pure and holy planet.

An orchestra of bodily instruments ensued: rumbles, crunches, squelches, I the conductor of such sounds. I followed the spurt of rouge that did fountain out from that beautifully busted bugle. A moment in time that can never be replicated ladies and gents, something real, something felt, something marked in the chronicles of this chap's tale. And so it ends, such a transient work of art, a tear may escape my eyeball but instead I did depart, fucked off sharpish.

I feel like I must lock horns in my life, assert one's authority through fights and fisticuffs. I shall always batter and spank and stomp out my woes for that is all I know. Not one soul has taught me another way. I mean, what do you expect, ey? When one must grow up on such an estate? I mean, let's get one thing straight, this devil I play, didn't you create? So don't be piercing holes through my skin with yah looks of disgust. Oh 'Blush, blush thou lump of foul deformity'. Get fucked. I'm off to the pub.

Glug.

Glug.

Glug.

TERRENCE *turns blind drunk before our very eyes and bowls into the flat.*

Scene Seven

End of a Hard Day's Graft

TERRENCE. Kelly! I'm home, get thine self to the
bedchamber, face down and ass to the gods, for this silly sod
is pissed and be in need of a vessel to dump all the hardships
of this taxing day. What say you!

Ey?

Kel?

Babe!

KELLY. He saunters in like fucking Achilles of the Trojan
War, thou shall not defeat me for I am immortal! He thinks
in that peabrain of his, clutching hold of his manhood as
though it's his prize for whatever dastardly deed he hath
done that day. I receive a solid smack on the ass, he flicks
his gaze towards our boudoir, thus we do depart from the
living room where Grandad's watching the soaps, Tel says
in his most deeply tone:

TERRENCE. Whatever you want tonight my lady, I shall lick
one's minge then hop to the high road and get you a doner
kebab and chips… if that is what you wish.

KELLY. Well, it ain't never gunna be caviar and Kama Sutra
with this mong now is it…

We wrap ourselves into crisp clean sheets, Terrence moves
across my body in an ungodly state of flux, I stretch my arms
out wide as he finds my prize and gets to work.

Covered up by bedsheets, TERRENCE *proceeds to try and
pleasure* KELLY *with his mouth.*

Oh Terry you god, you bringer of joy… Get up here now…
Oh come on, quick, before Grandad wants his dinner!

The pair begin to have sex, loudly. Until TERRENCE
unexpectedly grinds to a halt…

Oh for fuck's sake!

TERRENCE. Oh dear…

KELLY. That ain't what I want to ear…

TERRENCE. Reckon Grandad's got a score?

KELLY. What for?

TERRENCE. Well I was done, and still firmly inside your
    angelic cunt.

KELLY. What be the problem? You wrapped up right?

TERRENCE. When, to do that, did I have the poxy time?

KELLY. Oh you bloody twat!

TERRENCE. Oi!

KELLY. How can you forget that?

TERRENCE. You was rushing me!

KELLY. Don't be starting fuckery!

TERRENCE. Don't point at me.

KELLY. I'll throttle thee!

TERRENCE. Fuck offa me.

KELLY. I could kill!

TERRENCE. Why ain't you on the bleedin pill?

KELLY. Coz out my pockets money does not spill!

TERRENCE. Oh, shut –

KELLY. Don't!

TERRENCE. Your –

KELLY. Fucking –

TERRENCE. Mouth!

KELLY. Start! Your tone sends daggers right through my bones
    sometimes Terrence. You are –

TERRENCE. Will!

KELLY. Doing!

TERRENCE. You!

KELLY. My!

TERRENCE. Just!

KELLY. Head!

TERRENCE. Fuck!

KELLY. In!

TERRENCE. Off! I swear to fucking god!

KELLY. What!

TERRENCE. I'll kick!

KELLY. I'll rip!

TERRENCE. Your ass –

KELLY. Your dick!

TERRENCE. So hard!

KELLY. Right off!

TERRENCE. You'll cry!

KELLY. I'll laugh! Ha!

TERRENCE. Kelly – Don't get lary.

KELLY. Don't stare at me!

TERRENCE. You raising –

KELLY. My voice?

TERRENCE. Yeh –

KELLY. I am.

TERRENCE. Well I can too –

KELLY. Ooooo!

> KELLY *mocks* TERRENCE's *twitching eyeball for the audience.*

TERRENCE. Fuck you!

KELLY. Fuck you!

TERRENCE. I'm done.

KELLY. Go on!

TERRENCE. What?

KELLY. Fuck off.

TERRENCE. Where?

KELLY. Out.

TERRENCE. Now?

KELLY. Yeh.

TERRENCE. Fine.

KELLY. Right.

TERRENCE. Bye.

They freeze, both absolutely livid with one another. Tony Bennett's 'Rags to Riches' begins. They kiss and make up, GRANDAD bursts onto stage, singing over Bennett.

Scene Eight

Ford Thunderbird 1955

'Rags to Riches' cuts as though the record has skipped,
GRANDAD*'s knee is playing up and he leans on the chair at*
the side of the stage.

GRANDAD. When I die, I wanna go like my grandfather did,
in his sleep, not screaming like the passengers on his bus.

The fella what invented throat lozenges died last week.
There was no coffin at the funeral.

Fancied myself across the pond in the Big Apple I did, would
have got by just fine over there, oh yeh, had meself some
tasty bird, rolled on the wheels of a silver Ford Thunderbird
1955, rubbed one's shoulders with Old Blue Eyes, what a
time to be alive that would have been for a geezer working
the circuits down East. I would have stacked one's dollar
bills into a wedge and held them tightly with a nice silver
money-clip, produced it from the creamiest dinner jacket this
side of Manhattan and tipped whoever did greet me and my
American honeys with their pearly whites. Oh yeh, this
geezer would have done just fine, handsomely overseas.
How lucky can one guy be...

I kissed her and she kissed me,
Like a fella once said ain't that a kick in the head...

My grandad got his tongue shot off in the First World War...
but he don't talk about it.

No, no, but honestly I'll never forget what my old
grandfather said before he kicked the bucket, it was, 'How
far do you think I can kick that bucket?'

Alas, my Yankee dreams did stay but dreams up here in this
visionary head of mine. For I fell madly in love right here in
London town. She would move about, spritely like, in The
Palm Tree just off the Roman Road, and I would stand
before her atop my podium and please these prancing ponies
with sounds of the jazzy fifties. She was a diamond, a tasty

little thing, an undivided darling. I tell you now; hearts did race for sweet Eliza. I asked for her hand atop the Eiffel Tower when we did split to Paris to fill our ears with jazz, our eyes with beauty and our hearts with adoration.

It be a while after that our affairs did dip, and I would catch Eliza as she did sip from bottles of gin when she thought no one be noticing. That enchanting little thing began to twist and contort, sallow was her skin, her hair wiry and thin.

Alas, twas the intoxicants that did see her off in the end, inebriated and sedated she slumped with a Marlboro between her fingers and it did set aflame our home, took sweet Eliza too.

I always said she'd go out in a blaze!

I tell ya, that little bird, she certainly knew how to light up a room…

And now, I reside here.

GRANDAD *takes a seat.*

The old king hath clambered into the mountain, took up the rocky throne and he shall meld with the jagged walls, wear his craggy crown and welcome his demons with a hardened chest. Yes, this cave in which I sit all day be my only comfort now. I do fill the space with vinyl records whenever I'm alone, stand tall and hold a tune with Sinatra, Bennett, Dean Martin, all my beloveds, crackling through the speakers. I do like my residence, twas mine and mine alone, but share it I must with these unpleasant little scruffs. Alas, tis my granddaughter's fella and one must hold one's tongue. But, I wish for one sunny morn to wake from a steady slumber and see that they have fled, left me to my little piece of the past to build it as I wish, fill it with memories of sweet Eliza, us in our Ford Thunderbird, ah yes I did digress with the unpleasantries that did transpire. I did not get to the Big Apple no, but me and my sweetheart did save for that dashing motor and we brought the apple home.

The big raucous finale to 'Rags to Riches' plays out as GRANDAD *remembers the past.*

Scene Nine

Fight Night

The first line interrupts GRANDAD*'s ponderous end. His chair will remain the centre of attention and the family will invade his space, the 'big fight' is on, anarchic energy splatters the stage.*

This scene is fast. Excitement causes lines to be crashing into one another.

REISS. Tel! Five minutes till the fight, chuck Grandad off his chair! LESSAVIT!

TERRENCE *bursts onto stage, his bullish energy disgruntles* GRANDAD *who fidgets in his armchair.*

TERRENCE. Right! Old man! Get thine self off that fievin arse and make haste to the offie fore there ain't but two tinnies left in the refrigerator and it's fight night on the telly! Been waiting months for this rumble let me tell thee!

REISS *enters with a carrier bag of beers.*

REISS. No need to take flight you soppy old bag o'bones for I just finished a shift and I come bearing gifts. Take a swig of this bruvva.

REISS *hands* TERRENCE *a can, they cheer 'Fight Night!' and then rip them open and drink.*

KELLY. Fish and chips! Savaloy for Reiss and a pot a Royal Navy for you Grandad –

GRANDAD. Cheers me dear!

KELLY. – and before thou bites off my ear, twas rammed and I forgot your pickled onion, an honest mistake.

GRANDAD. Fuck sake.

KELLY. What did I say!

REISS. Will youse pipe down! Tel and I like the build-up.

GRANDAD. Who's fighting?

TERRENCE. You will be – for your life – if you keep yapping over the good bits!

GRANDAD. Thou art command a bit of respect you toerag!

REISS. Why is this box so catastrophically bad?

GRANDAD. Oi! I've ad that since you were swimming about in your old man's sack –

KELLY. Grandad!

GRANDAD. I ave!

TERRENCE. Will you shut ya noise and listen! This ain't no fender-bender minor match-up people, this ain't no tickling tournament, some frolicsome game, no, no, no mate. This be a blood-soaked battle between gods of the flogging kind. Where two machines collide in unadulterated power of the muscle and the mind. Love the fucking boxing, me!

GRANDAD. Will you shift out the way of the poxy TV!

TERRENCE. Oi, I've got a big bet on, me!

GRANDAD. Well I can't bleedin well see!

REISS. Pray tell bruvva, how much has thou spunked?

TERRENCE. A score, the big fella to fall on his arse in the four.

REISS. Cor, ain't sure.

TERRENCE. Five large if it lands.

REISS. Yeah but –

TERRENCE. Our man's got quick hands. Have faith little bruv. Kel, pinch a tinnie from behind thine self darlin.

KELLY. There's Stella or Pils.

TERRENCE. Tonight I shall suckle on the teat of Madame Artois…

REISS. Look! Geezer's coming out, he ain't fucking about is he! Size of his head!

KELLY. Crikey…

TERRENCE. Let there be bloodshed!

The family whip round and descend sharply, JAMAL rises, from behind them, staring up at his 'ceiling' bashing a broom upwards.

JAMAL. Keep tha noise down or, I swear, mans' dead!

JAMAL switches with the family who are back with turbulent, riotous energy.

GRANDAD. What's his name then?

REISS. Shut it Grandad it's about to begin.

The sound of a 'DING! DING!' The group follow the action, twitching with every muscle flexed.

REISS *and* TERRENCE. Use ya jab you slag!

In unison the gang wince as one of the fighters receives an almighty blow to the stomach.

REISS. Ooooh, right in the gut!

KELLY. Surprised he ain't chucked up.

REISS *and* TERRENCE. Get up!

The gang's heads become a chorus of cringes and swerves.

TERRENCE. Come on you bastard! It ain't difficult!

GRANDAD. Like to see you get in there…

Their heads follow the punches together. An excitement building until they all cheer!

They whip around again and JAMAL stands tall, bashing his ceiling with a broom just like before.

JAMAL. I swear, I will kill thee! My mum's tryna sleep…

The action swings round again and we are back in the living room with the family.

KELLY. Ow long do these things last, bit yawnful ain't it.

GRANDAD. Back in my day you could saunter down Bethnal Green and chuck a few quid on two geezers going at it bare-knuckled!

KELLY. They've just been pissin about for the last ten minutes.

TERRENCE. It's an art form, there's a science to it!

KELLY. What do you know about bloody science!

REISS and TERRENCE *cheer as an almighty left-hook is landed.*

REISS. It's the fourth Tel, fingers firmly crossed bruvva!

The family get closer and closer to the TV set. TERRENCE *and* REISS *are on their knees. Suddenly the brothers burst into cheer!*

He's out!

TERRENCE. You fucking beauty!

KELLY. Ey?

REISS. What a touch!

The brothers hug victorious.

TERRENCE. Kel, I've won! That's five hundred notes babe!

KELLY. Shutcha mouth?

TERRENCE. I ain't pissin about!

KELLY'*s disbelief turns into a great, big grin and* TERRENCE *gives her a great, big kiss.*

I'll collect it first thing. Then, whisk thee away to the fanciest eating place we can behold babe!

REISS. Dough like that I should hope we're all going!

TERRENCE. Sod off!

KELLY. Oh come on, the lot of us ascending on a load of poshies, be a right laugh!

GRANDAD. I'm havin' a steak with Béarnaise sauce and those chips what get cooked hundred times and a big fat grilled tomato!

REISS. How can thee be getting all stiff over food when you've just polished off that cod and chips?

GRANDAD. I like my grub.

REISS. Yeah, we know, it be you pinching all the bloody bread every morning!

GRANDAD. No it ain't!

TERRENCE. Will you shut up! We'll all go you ugly gits!

KELLY. Oi!

TERRENCE. Not you, you're gorgeous!

TERRENCE *kisses* KELLY.

KELLY. Don't think I've ever seen a monkey in real life! Five large...

The gang erupt. They start to sing 'Rags to Riches' loudly, leaving the stage in the process, JAMAL *cuts through the chanting –*

JAMAL. I swear to god make noise some more, I'll bust your jaw and let slip the dogs or war!

Scene Ten

Hellfire

JAMAL *is left alone, centre stage, staring up at the gang's flat. He composes himself and notices the auditorium judging his violent spat of verbals.*

JAMAL. Do I bore thee? With incessant anger and poisonous disposition. Or perhaps I be frightful, my contentious survival through this wasteland rattles you? I clutch on to my woes like chains around satanic hounds, foaming through razored teeth, snarling at my foes... for nobody really knows me. I be another villain just like Terrence that primitive hunk of meat. I be stamped offender, culprit, delinquent as soon as I put one foot from my quarters. Well, friends, Romans, countrymen lend me your ears. I come to bury this stigma, not praise it. For I have secrets, unknown to my brothers, that would wash away my esteemed act I work so tiresomely to portray, the one which roofs my mother and I. If I were not born in hellfire I would be so very unlike this devilish masquerade of mine.

I ain't never won no fight, nor do I see the pleasantries in such physical extremities, to be honest the thought makes me feel quite faint, I ain't never been hit aside a rounder's ball in the eye on the school pitch. Told all the boys I wrestled this older head, that tears shed from his ducts like a schoolboy bitch. And did you see how quickly I did pillage that offie? Had to be in and out sharpish for I had never had to hold my asshole clenched so tightly.

Alas, I'm gassed when the Great Bake Off gets rollin, and I just love strolling, you know? Long walks to clear my head, they're the best. And who gives a fuck if I'm still a virgin at twenty-four?

I have spilt to much...

Fuck you looking at me for? I will strike down upon thee with great vengeance and furious anger! Wanker...

It troubles me so, keeps me from sleep, this unreachable feat
that I, me, Jamal, the hardest bastard on this block, ain't
never had a girl on the end of his cock...

Now it ain't that I must exert oneself to court the opposing
sex and fail in my attempts, no, no, no, I garner attention,
accumulate many digits, I've kissed like six girls, touched
the odd pair of tits too, I ain't no rookie.

Once, one Saturday eve down in Dalston, right? I swept
through the night with this beautiful, classy angel named
'Chantelle' a blonde bombshell of a 'gel'. Fingers entwined,
bellies full of wine and ales, we did depart the bar in which
we found each other's eyes and, sprite like through the neon
night, she led me to a darkly alley round the back of The Rio,
without one single utterance she dropped to her knees and
told me, 'I bet thee has a belter of a cock!' In a flurry of
unease, as Chantelle did burp the kebab she had devoured
that eve, I carefully moved her aside and did flee that fiddly
scene round the back by The Rio's bins. See for all my sins,
for all my nasty wrongdoings, I am but a boy, to scared to try
anything that don't fit into the life I lead.

But that don't mean you can call me a pussy!

Sorry... I can be horrid.

I long to live a fruitful life; taste the juices that are there for
the taking. This irksome gnawing at my chest, my stomach,
my head, stunts me from breaking free from the life I, right
now, do lead. You see, it's me that creates this secondary
personality, the scarecrow I pitch up and decide to be, the
dog that aids in people's travesties...

But I do believe that one man in his time plays many parts.
And through the tempestuous wind and the unceasing
clattering the waves bring most men will come up breathing,
scuffed and scraped, chipped away at, but nonetheless men.
When I die, be it a long time from here, I want to grin and
bare my chipped teeth, covered in blood and stories. I will
look upon my sons and daughters that I will have raised like

almighty pillars for our descendants and let them run fingers
down my weathered body and the last words I will speak,
whilst still grinning those gnarled teeth, I have lived... And
I've got to have had sex.

There is a mighty knocking coming from offstage. Then a
booming voice, it's JAMAL's mum. She screams for him to
clean his room, he runs off.

Scene Eleven

Pregnant on the Front Line

KELLY. There's a Kit Kat Chunky behind the sofa and it's
melted into the bleedin carpet, what div hath I to blame! For
christ almighty's sake!

To me, life is but a projection of somewhere else, like a
simulator upon a computer screen, some godly figure has
created this place and that dozy bastard has fucked off, left
this world to run a riot, unpaused and unlorded thus creating
havoc, pits like this down here. Perhaps we should stay
unmoved and twiddle one's thumbs until our god returns,
and whence he bares witness to the utter mess he hath left
behind he shall not dither to delete us all. Maybe I be
blinded, by the heap in which I sink, I mean some people
have it cushty, right? Some people actually love their lives.

It was precisely two months after mine and Tel's miniature
war atop our bedding that I got to thinking these deeply
thoughts.

They swelled, frothed and advanced through my brain
certifying myself insane with quick trips to the interweb to
diagnose this psychological change, my moods did sway
from elation to pure fucking rage every minute of every
shit-piss day.

Two moons back the family sat upon miniature thrones about a table, christly-like, with all breads and wines. The five hundred large Terrence did win shoved us into this grotto of Italian delights where my bloke, fistfull of pound notes, did take upon the role of some grand duke of twat-town ordering the servers about, his discordant tone belching out:

TERRENCE. 'You got any olives pal?'

KELLY. and –

TERRENCE. 'Ow much garlic bread dost thou get on one portion mate.'

KELLY. I felt rather out of place. Thou art began to feel rather irate. Flush in the face. Feeling like I'd swallowed a fucking bowling ball my ovaries did pulsate. All these decadent assholes about us in twos and threes with lizard-like tongues, cuts of meat hanging from their Hampstead Heaths, spitting loudly bout their overdone fucking beef and boards of matured cheese. I said: 'Terrence, pray, I would like to leave.' He did reply, face gauged with steak and red wine, 'What dya mean?'

That is when I lost my rag. Trapped I felt, within this cage of contemptible wealth.

Thought I saw some old bird dressed up to the eyeballs in French brands give us lot an almighty gawk up and down so I spat, '*Problem? Twat!*' We were politely asked to leave as Grandad did proceed to throw a lump of unchewable meat over his shoulder, slapping some fella on the cheek. We were ushered out and thrown onto the concrete streets to get the 243 back home, East. Fucking embarrassing to say the least.

I decided upon hormones for the reason toward my outburst, my most ladily parts fucking with my brain... but no bloodily welcome came. Therefore, I pissed on a stick I bought at the shops and it told me I be pregnant. Perfect, just sodding perfect. Cheers Terrence, yeh, thanks for that, twat! It took me a week to tell the shit-heap but tell him I did:

*TERRENCE enters picking 'stuff' out of his belly button.
He finds what he had been digging around for and eats it.*

Terrence, I'm pregnant, we're having a kid...

TERRENCE. Oh shit.

KELLY. What's that?

TERRENCE. Well, Kel, I mean, we don't even feed the fucking cat...

*TERRENCE slaps KELLY on the bum and leaves,
whistling.*

KELLY. Hats off that took the crown for being the crappiest spew of syllables he had spat in a long time.

A football is shoved up KELLY's top, she is now very much pregnant.

I grew at an almighty rate, a miniature mountain, the Everest to my other lumps atop my body. Posture was knackered, my back ached and I seemed to stagger about with bowed legs like I'd shit myself. A right pickle I was in, sweating, breathing, heavy thoughts, seething over Reiss's mess, stressed when Grandad opened his chops and Tel the almighty, the commander of this microscopic siege, did use his wooden horse to enter the City of Troy, spunk out his swimmers and capture my egg, almighty dickhead! If he so much did lift a finger wrongly I might just rip his head right off!

Funny innit, what awakens one's eyes sometimes. God hath given me all this precious time down here on this pretty rock and I be sitting on my arse most of it hidden to life's fantastical sights, stuck in this dank and bleakly prison. I have not lived a fruitful life... And now the rest of mine will have its time snatched away by what will come screeching out from this bump and into this battlefield which I have beared my whole existence. Christ, be I like my kindred mother I shall, as likely as not, take one's leave of this babe and fuck off to sunny Mallorca with a plumber named Rodrigo, stinking of Yves Saint Laurent, driving about in a fucking rotten yellow

Porsche, ignoring my phone calls and cackling all the way to that dirty little island... or something utterly shitty like that. That vile, sour-faced cow.

These vexing visions I cast within this worrisome nut did get me out the house, a brisk strut across greenery and trees would force me to breathe, when I happened upon a poster, in big letters spread across the top it did say: SINGERS WANTED, A HUNDRED POUND A DAY. Unsure and ready to walk I was stunted by a kick, right there where the kid did sit. *Little shit.* I rubbed meself better and went to leave but another little boot did proceed. 'What dya want?' I screamed like some mad cow into my belly button right there on the street. And then I swear to ya, on my nana's grave, a sailing note, swift like a breeze, did speak to me from the depths of my belly. Just one word came from this life-giving lump and swum the flood of air unto my earholes:

SING.

And well that was fucking it, my unborn kid be telling me to do it, sing it fucking spoke, can you believe it! This be some *Hello* magazine shit. I ripped off the bottom bit dangling there with all the details and I exercised my abilities in the abode, when nobody was about. I would close my eyes and belt out heavenly notes...

KELLY *breaks into song, lost in her own little world, her favourite tune plays out and she is happy for a moment.*

REISS. Tel, someone's kicking a pig up the arse in the bathroom!

TERRENCE *and* REISS *erupt into laughter.* KELLY *notices.*

KELLY. I swear to god you devils, you fucking imps, piss off fore I lose my rag!

I left in a flurry, my belly so big and tender now this irksome kid was ready to shoot out. I made the 149 into Shoreditch and found the little place whereby I would bounce sounds around the room. Inside, two shady pairs of eyes did sit

before a desk, I stood on a mark and myself I did address.
Kel, I said. Then I opened my gob to make beauteous noise
but nothing came out, for something else had come about,
my legs felt damp, then they did feel soaked, for – Sod's law
– my waters had broke.

KELLY *doubles over with contractions, the scene quickly*
changes into the family at a hospital. KELLY is pushed
awkwardly into the front row of the audience, she uses the
audience members to prop herself up and her legs are
opened wide. A Nigerian doctor who looks an awful lot like
JAMAL *squats down between her legs.*

JAMAL. What I need you to do madam, is to try and push.

KELLY. I am bloody pushing, christ!

JAMAL. Okay, if we could make some space for the lady!

EVERYONE. You what? We wanna watch!

KELLY. Just all fuck off!

JAMAL. I see a head.

TERRENCE. Boy or a girl?

GRANDAD. How can he tell from a soddin forehead!

TERRENCE. It'll ave long hair won't it!

JAMAL. Okay, okay, almost there, push!

KELLY. I force any more, my bowels will gush out and be over
the soddin floor!

JAMAL. More!

REISS. Go on Kelly!

TERRENCE. Thrust babe!

GRANDAD, *who has been beside her head, takes a quick*
look at the action.

GRANDAD. Well I wish I hadn't done that…

KELLY. Stay here you twat!

TERRENCE. Reiss please feast your eyes on this atrocity.

REISS. Jeez, that is monstrous, like truly horrifying.

TERRENCE. I don't know if I'll ever be the same again brother.

KELLY. Terrence you bastard!

JAMAL. Here we go, make way!

The DOCTOR *shuffles back away from the scene and holds his hands before him like he is about to catch a rugby ball. In an instant a football is fired out towards the* DOCTOR *who catches it whilst diving through the air. The family hold their breath. The* DOCTOR *slaps the baby and it start to cry. He turns with a huge grin on his face.*

It's a girl!

The gang pick KELLY *up and erupt into cheers, the baby is wrapped up and given to its mother. Everyone is shaking hands and very happy. They freeze in semicircle around* KELLY *who begins to sing to her little girl. As* KELLY *sings her final few notes, the rest of the cast begin to raise their arms, angelically. Though as she finishes they all stuff their fingers in their ears.*

The family exit the hospital and walk offstage.

TERRENCE *breaks off, he tries to light a cigarette, he is overwhelmed by the situation.*

REISS *also hangs back.*

Scene Twelve

The Ballad of the Hard Man

REISS. Bruvva, I need you to lend me your ears for a sec.

TERRENCE. Yeah, yeah. These hearing holes are all yours, go on what dya want?

REISS. It be like this bruv, promise you won't screw?

TERRENCE. Just voice it you pansy, come on, spit.

REISS. Well it be hard for me to say.

TERRENCE. Well brave it, sharpish.

REISS. I'm gay.

TERRENCE. Ey?

REISS. I'm gay, I like men brother.

TERRENCE. No you don't.

REISS. Yes, I do.

TERRENCE. Since when?

REISS. Since forever.

TERRENCE. Why ain't you said nuffin?

REISS. Fear, Terrence.

TERRENCE. What you talking about?

REISS. I'm scared mate!

TERRENCE. Of what?

REISS. You.

After a pause, REISS *leaves the stage,* TERRENCE *is left alone.*

TERRENCE. Be I a monster? Well? Confront me peerless world instruct and I will follow! Teach me, humanity, empathy, fucking clarity something to scrape of these crustaceans I carry. Not one of ye, can lift me from such a benighted travesty. Thou brother fears me! Thou brother fears me… My flesh and bone doth doubt my sympathy, does keep secrets

from me, does not seek counsel from me, and yet, I do not
take to with open arms and flood thou in compassion for
I worry my wisdom, it wears thin... I strangle with foolish
tuition. I love my brother, any which way he chooseth to be,
so why does he flee?

What is it about me that even family cannot unsee? Is it that
I''m mindless, thick with heat. That I carry great weight upon
my back. That I cannot help but be bad. Praps this pestilent
pressure I do pour upon my blood is my only pith. What else
might a man like me have? No dreams to be had. How can a
man like me be a fucking dad? A good man who teaches and
instils love and hope into a heart, not me. Me is the thunder
that gathers, me is the lightning that clouts and brings misery
about. Me is the beast that struts with steely chest. Me is the
one that smashed the bus stop, that spits and shouts and
lingers about, armed with cans of lager in hand. Me is the
ogre that you dare not see. The one that leads violence to
these streets. Me is the monster that hates your king and
queen, that lays about, eats, shits, sleeps and repeats and you
all fucking pay for me...

That be what you all see, at the very least. A witless ape that
does see and thus do. Well, just this, I ain't. I ain't no dog.
Some layabout, some freak show to which you thank your
gods you don't follow suit. You know not of what I have been
through, the whips and scorns of time, what life I have had to
fight and hear me now, be this not a tirade, some thick and
densely bluster, I ain't drunk, nor fucked up, but I will spit and
cuss until the dogged judge makes rotten fruit of me...

I long to be the shepherd of my family. I pray for some
wisdom to break through the heavens and strike me so that
I can sculpt this baby, hold it safely. I fear, that the life I hath
brought unto this rock will not want me, sense my
stupidity... Me and my stifling density, my bullish thuggery.
Just another loved one afraid of me... Another branch on the
family tree covered in sap from the disease that is yours
truly. Bonds of blood be the quintessence of life so why do
I try to drive mine southerly. God knows this must not be so.

Blackout.

Scene Thirteen

The End is Always Nigh

A flood of light drowns the stage. TERRENCE *is quickly pulled from his thoughts and into this new setting. A hubbub of construction noise envelops the whole theatre.*

TERRENCE. Oit, what's goin on? Ey? No I live ere, this is my block. No I won't hang on a minute pal, what's all this nonsense?

Everyone, in canons, charges out onto the stage, before them are construction workers breaking out all over the estate. The gang want answers. In a chorus, the gang move about the stage following the workers, picking their fights with some of them. KELLY *is holding her baby.*

KELLY. What fuckery does gird thee? Speak! Who be your guvna! Oh, I see... the geezer with his brightly crown and his coat of fluorescent clout. Come here, what say you!

TERRENCE. Ey? Ang on, wait, decant, what does thou mean, my family ain't a can of fucking baked beans!

KELLY. Will you let him speak!

GRANDAD. Shut that off or feel my wrath you great big git!

REISS. Mail from our council?

EVERYONE. We don't open that shit!

TERRENCE. What? No! Where would we bleedin go?

KELLY. We ain't got no one else to house us, don't you know I have a three-month-old babe!

The family are ushered backwards, disorderly and unfairly pushed back into the corner of the stage.

REISS. You best turn round mate!

JAMAL. Na, na, na hold your tongue blad! Man intends to throw man from his abode and call a grotty mattress at the leisure centre his home, what about my mum, she be unfit for a setting like that slum!

The gang rush over to the other side, keeping together, one little battalion, just like the Spartans.

REISS. That be the result if disaster hath struck, when really this is by your hands you cunt!

GRANDAD. This is unlawful! We bloody reside ere!

REISS. What say you? The block a bit of an eyesore is it, clearing out the vermin are ya? Bastard!

KELLY. And what be the outcome for us? Be it the streets? This is our home; we grew up on this block!

REISS. The people hath learnt of your dastardly deeds! You've been trying to clear us out for months! Admit it!

They chase down the workers.

TERRENCE. Listen to my brother he's the only one here talking some sense, smartest bloke I know...

REISS glances at his brother a little longer than intended, he is touched by this. Then, he snaps out of it and guns for the builders, the suits with hard hats and clipboards.

REISS. It was you who did plant those rats on to our estate.

GRANDAD. Yeh! No doubt a stinking plot, to corrode our block!

EVERYONE. Yeh!

KELLY. You won't get away with this, the people won't allow it!

TERRENCE, REISS and JAMAL whip round in anger, they huddle up and try to formulate a plot.

GRANDAD. Kel, darlin, what's going on? That's my whole life up there!

KELLY. I know, Grandad, we'll sort this out, I love ya, alright?

GRANDAD. Likewise gel! They can't do this, surely? Ascend no more! Clear off!

TERRENCE shoots forward to centre stage.

TERRENCE. You ever set foot ere before pal?

JAMAL. What be your wager? Fifty K in thou's back burner to tear us down is it? Share a moment to think about the atrocity of this act!

REISS. Arriving in your big mechanical beast, blueprints covered in cash signs, raising your thumb gladiatorial-like, to watch it bash and trash our lives, who the fuck are you mate!

The gang are pushed back by the workers, they shout and complain. TERRENCE *intervenes.*

TERRENCE. Whoa, whoa! Is thee mental? Step one more foot I dare ya! It's witless bastards like you that form our fury!

EVERYONE. YEH!

TERRENCE. We don't scare easy.

EVERYONE. Pleased to be rowdy!

TERRENCE. We'll surround thee, crush thee like a thousand tsunamis, we're a fucking army!

KELLY. Our battle cries will carry through the streets whilst we bleed and our children weep.

JAMAL. We won't fucking sleep.

GRANDAD. I'll chain thine own self to these concrete streets.

JAMAL. Try take our homes, come forth, ye wretched dogs, bombastic sods with insidious plots.

REISS. Think not of wads to fill the pockets of fake demigods, think upon us, the people.

TERRENCE. What do you leer upon and not see? We are the roots that tie, like thick trees, this shit-piece together. Don't you see! We're poor round here, take all that you fancy! Go on! You shall not end our reign of these streets. The East is ours and forever will be! Once more unto the breach dear friends, once more!

EVERYONE. Come and ave a go if you think you're ard enough!

CLAP, CLAP, CLAP!

Come and ave a go if you think you're ard enough!

CLAP, CLAP, CLAP!

The lads look ready to pounce. KELLY *comes forward.*

KELLY. This 'bombsite' that we do breath upon, that others so
easily avert, is home, tis a place I've felt safe for many a
year. These walls keep some real good folk from the cold!
Folk not consumed by our rocks narcissistic mess, they are
some of the best.

Will you just look upon us all for a moment, what chance
hath you granted us? To be uprooted, shifted, sifted through
a system so's that prosperity be a fairytale to us, should we
bow down and be herded about from pen to pen until we
profitably drop like flies. Be it no surprise to find we are
merely cannon fodder for a governmental side that seems not
to give a monkey's. You take everything from us, every
single fucking day, our energy, our health, our warmth, our
educations, our freedom. Be gone; give us this one day of
victory. Drop your defences, stand down and remember this
moment. We are the people and we shall hold this day.

The gang unify and stand strong.

Mozart's 'Requiem' begins.

TERRENCE. Life at the bottom ain't so pretty…

REISS. It's earthy and moist, dank and sometimes depressive.

JAMAL. It's cramped and stuffy, a hole which deepens with
every clawed attempt to escape.

KELLY. And yet, struggle we might, rock bottom is merely the
foundations we can build upon.

TERRENCE. You see, when dirty hands you have all your life,
contentment comes in many a shape and size.

GRANDAD. A basic life will do nice, just don't prod us and
we'll be fine.

REISS. Get off your arse and have a look about.

TERRENCE. Find a bird.

KELLY. Play husbands and wives.

GRANDAD. Get a cat, maybe a dog.

JAMAL. Find a job.

TERRENCE. Watch the box.

REISS. Down the pub.

JAMAL. Sink a few.

KELLY. Quick shag.

GRANDAD. Pop out a kid.

REISS. Teach it to kick,

    Teach it to spit.

TERRENCE. Get old,

JAMAL. Get fat,

KELLY. Get ill.

REISS. Buy crap.

TERRENCE. Buy more crap.

GRANDAD. Save up, go away.

JAMAL. Somewhere hot,

KELLY. Probably Spain.

REISS. Burn a bit,

TERRENCE. Sit about.

JAMAL. Make complaints.

GRANDAD. Vote or don't,

KELLY. Either way,

REISS. It's all the same.

TERRENCE. Rainy days,

JAMAL. Sunny days,

GRANDAD. Chinese takeaways.

KELLY. Retire.

REISS. Expire.

TERRENCE. Oh for this virile eloquence shall burn so
brightly! We be the heroes and the heroines, we be the
villains and the monsters, we be characters grown from a
story of grit! Of darkness and light, we be but players in this
life! So do not forget our tales of woe, these outpours of
uberly bloated tongue for it be us who shall pick up this rock
and heave and huff through earth and dust, break and snap,
put out one's back so that others do live... cushty.

The End.

The Pleasance Theatre

The Pleasance Theatre Trust co-produced *Flesh and Bone* at the Edinburgh Festival Fringe in 2017. Unpolished Theatre were recipients of the Pleasance's 2017 Charlie Hartill Special Reserve Fund, set up in 2004 in honour of Charlie, who died that year. For over thirty years the Pleasance has been celebrated as one of the most successful theatre organisations at the Edinburgh Festival Fringe and on the London fringe. The Pleasance provides a vital stepping-stone for thousands of artists and companies, a place for theatre makers both on and off stage to take risks and develop their work. The Charlie Hartill Special Reserve Fund is one of many ways that The Pleasance supports artistic ambition within Pleasance Futures, our artist development programme.

Eastlake Productions

Established in 2001 by a nine-year-old Geordie lad, with enormous dreams, limitless ambition and a wild imagination, Eastlake Productions is now one of London's most prominent Fringe producers.

In 2017 alone they mounted fourteen productions including the critically acclaimed *This Is Not Culturally Significant*, internationally acclaimed Frank Simatra and multiple Offie-nominated *The Tailor Made Man* plus an incredibly successful Edinburgh Fringe programme of eight shows. In 2018 they have continued to support emerging companies and artists, staging work across London, most recently at The Bunker Theatre.

Eastlake Productions is a sister company of Theatre N16, also run by Jamie Eastlake. Theatre N16 was set up at the start of 2015 to be a stomping group for new companies and to 'give hope to theatre-makers who had been priced our of making work' by offering the lowest overheads on the London fringe. It is one of the few London venues to have signed the Equity Fringe Agreement to guarantee fair pay for all creatives working in the venue. In the last three years it has had homes in Stoke Newington, Balham and now in Tottenham Hale, staging 178 productions from 132 different theatre companies involving over 1500 artists and over 28,000 audiences through their doors. Nearly half of the productions started at Theatre N16 have led to transfers to other venues and tours. The theatre has been the first professional credit for over two hundred new performers.

'There's a clear passion radiating from this venue'
View from the Gods

Artistic Director Jamie Eastlake
Executive Producer Richard Jenkinson
Associate Producer Ellie Gauge

SOHO THEATRE

Soho Theatre is London's most vibrant venue for new theatre, comedy and cabaret. We occupy a unique and vital place in the British cultural landscape. Our mission is to produce new work, discover and nurture new writers and artists, and target and develop new audiences. We work with artists in a variety of ways, from full producing of new plays, to co-producing new work, working with associate artists and presenting the best new emerging theatre companies that we can find.

We have numerous artists on attachment and under commission, including Soho Six and a thriving Young Company of writers and comedy groups. We read and see hundreds of scripts and shows a year.

'the place was buzzing, and there were queues all over the building as audiences waited to go into one or other of the venue's spaces....young, exuberant and clearly anticipating a good time.' Guardian.

We attract over 240,000 audience members a year at Soho Theatre, at festivals and through our national and international touring. We produced, co-produced or staged over 35 new plays in the last 12 months.

As an entrepreneurial charity and social enterprise, we have created an innovative and sustainable business model. We maximise value from Arts Council England and philanthropic funding, contributing more to government in tax and NI than we receive in public funding.

Registered Charity No: 267234

Soho Theatre, 21 Dean Street
London W1D 3NE
Admin 020 7287 5060
Box Office 020 7478 0100

OPPORTUNITIES FOR WRITERS AT SOHO THEATRE

We are looking for unique and unheard voices – from all backgrounds, attitudes and places.

We want to make things you've never seen before.

Alongside workshops, readings and notes sessions, there are several ways writers can connect with Soho Theatre. You can

- **enter** our prestigious biennial competition the **Verity Bargate Award** just as **Vicky Jones** did in 2013 with her Award-winning first play The One.

- **participate** in our nine month long **Writers' Labs programme**, where we will take you through a three-draft process.

- **submit** your script to submissions@sohotheatre.com where your play will go directly to our Artistic team

- **invite** us to see your show via coverage@sohotheatre.com

We consider every submission for production or any of the further development opportunities.

sohotheatre.com

Keep up to date:

sohotheatre.com/mailing-list
@sohotheatre all social media

www.nickhernbooks.co.uk

facebook.com/nickhernbooks

twitter.com/nickhernbooks